Sharks

Izabella Hearn with Alex Hearn

Level 2

Series Editors: Andy Hopkins and Jocelyn Potter

Pearson Education Limited
Edinburgh Gate, Harlow,
Essex CM20 2JE, England
and Associated Companies throughout the world.

ISBN: 978-1-2921-9602-2

This edition first published by Pearson Education Ltd 2014

7 9 10 8

Illustrations by David Shephard and Oxford Illustrators & Designers

Set in 12/15.5pt A. Garamond
Printed in Great Britain by Ashford Colour Press Ltd.
SWTC/02

Published by Pearson Education Ltd

Acknowledgements

The publisher would like to thank the following for their kind permission
to reproduce their photographs:

(Key: b-bottom; c-centre; l-left; r-right; t-top)

Alamy Images: blickwinkel 16, ImageSelect 44; **American Scientist Magazine**: Diagram of hammerhead swimming away and back to seamount: Figure 8 in Klimley, Richert & Jorgensen (2005) Home of Blue Water Fish. In : American Scientist, vol 93 p42-42. 38; **FLPA Images of Nature**: Chris Newbert / Minden Pictures 5, Colin Marshall 32,33, Fred Bavendam / Minden Pictures 41, Malcolm Schuyl 22b, Mike Parry 24, Norbert Wu 25b, Pascal Kobeh 17t, Reinhard Dirscherl 11, 12b, 21b, 25t; **Getty Images**: Peter Williams 16b, Visuals Unlimited 17b; **Imagemore Co., Ltd**: 21t; **Marco Flagg**: 22c; **Science Photo Library Ltd**: L. NEWMAN & A. FLOWERS 39; **Shutterstock.com**: Greg Amptman 23t, Lawrence Cruciana 10, 12t, MP cz 4, Photosky 23bl

Contents

1.1 What's the book about?

1 Look at the picture. What do you think?

- **a** How many different sharks are there in our oceans? ....
- **b** How long do sharks live? ....
- **c** How many teeth can sharks have? ....
- **d** How long can sharks be? ....

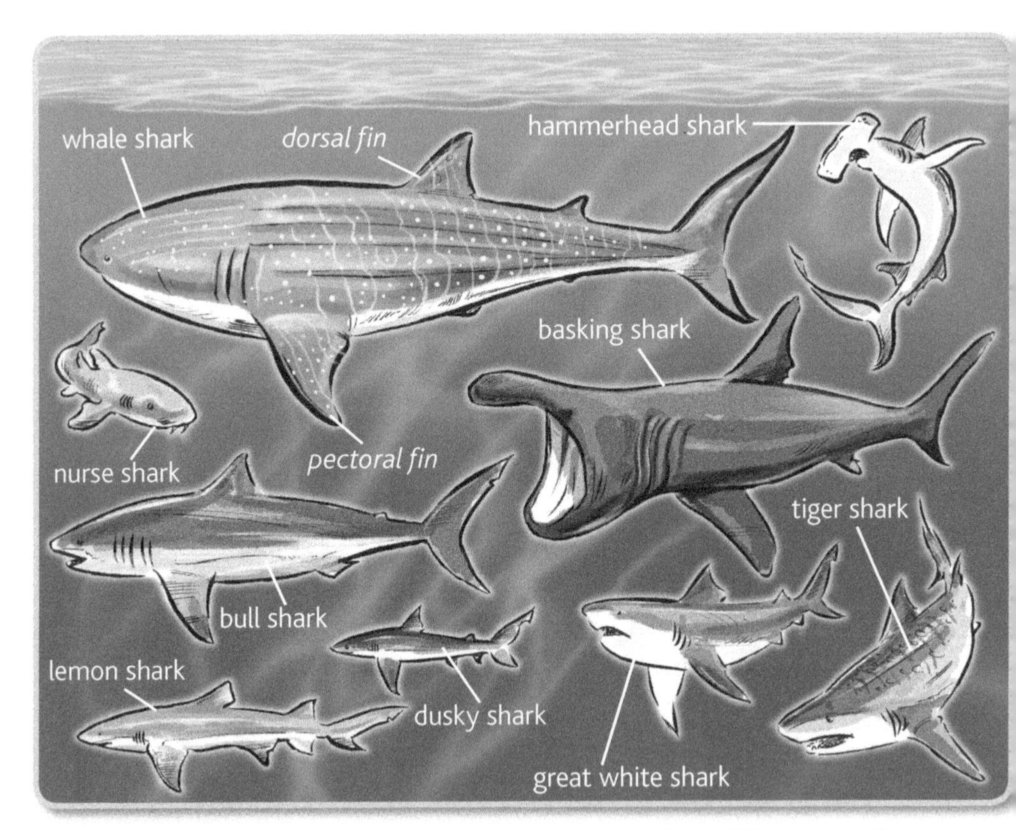

2 Choose two sharks from 1.1 above. How are they different? Talk to other students.

1.2 What's first?

Discuss these questions. What do you think?

1. In the first chapter Freddy is unhappy about the future of sharks. Why?
2. What problems do sharks have? Write notes in your notebook.

CHAPTER 1

A Family Problem

"We can get the money, Ed! You know that."
"Oh, no! Not shark finning! There has to be a better way!"

Freddy ran into the house with a letter in his hand. It was important and he wanted to speak to his parents.

"Where is everybody?" he shouted.

Freddy's mother came out of the kitchen. "We're eating, Freddy. You're late, so we started without you. What's happening?"

Freddy followed his mother and sat down at the table. His father looked at him with tired eyes.

"So, what's the problem?" he asked.

Freddy read them the letter: "*Dear Mr. Mendez*—listen to this!—*there is a place for you at Northcoast College in February next year ...*"

Ed looked at his son. There was a big smile on his face. "That's wonderful!"

"Yes ... but ..." Freddy didn't look happy. "There's a problem, Dad.

There aren't any free places. Everybody has to pay now."

Freddy's mother looked at her husband. "We can get the money, Ed! You know that."

"Oh, no! Not **shark finning**! There has to be a better way!" thought Freddy.

Freddy and his parents lived on a small **island** in the Pacific Ocean. Ed was a **fisherman**. He worked very hard but he had little money. He had a small boat and usually he only caught fish. But sometimes he went out with other fishermen and they looked for sharks. They could get a lot of money for shark fins.

In some countries, people make **soup** from the fins. Fishermen find sharks and cut off their fins. Then they throw the sharks back into the ocean. Sharks can't swim without fins, so they die, slowly. Every year, fishermen kill about 80 **million** sharks, and many kinds are now **endangered**.

And now Ed had to find the money to pay for Freddy's years at college. Freddy and his mother knew about the shark finning trips and they sometimes helped Ed. They didn't like it but it was the only way. Or was it?

Freddy went for a long walk on the beach. He loved his home, the color of the sky, the sound of the ocean, and the wonderful animal life around him. He wanted to study and then to **protect** this beautiful place. He couldn't go to college without money, but he didn't want the ocean to lose more sharks.

Later that evening, Freddy stopped at the Birdsong Hotel. He wanted

shark finning /ˈʃɑrk ˌfɪnɪŋ/ (n) When people go *shark finning*, they take only the sharks' fins. They leave the sharks in the water and sell the fins.
island /ˈaɪlənd/ (n) An *island* is a place with water all around it.
fisherman /ˈfɪʃɚmən/ (n) A *fisherman* catches fish.
soup /sup/ (n) *Soup* is a kind of food, with meat, fish, or vegetables in it. You can drink it from a cup, or you eat it with a spoon.
million /ˈmɪlyən/ (n) 1,000 x 1,000 is a *million*.
endangered /ɪnˈdeɪndʒɚd/ (v) An *endangered* animal is one of the last animals of its kind. The lives of these animals are in *danger*.
protect /prəˈtɛkt/ (v) When life is dangerous for people or animals, we try to *protect* them.

to talk to somebody and his friend Pam worked there. The hotel was her father's and his family helped with the work. Freddy saw Pam, but she was busy. He found a chair next to a young woman. She had a book in her hand and he could see photos of hammerhead sharks.

"Hi! Are you interested in sharks?" he asked.

She smiled at him. "Of course! I came here because I want to **dive**. Are you Freddy?"

"Yes, that's right," says Freddy, "and you are …?"

"My name's Kristin. I'm from California. I'm a friend of Pam. We saw you on the beach yesterday."

Freddy thought about the beach and the sharks.

"And do you swim with sharks?" he asked.

"Yes, I do!" answered Kristin. "I swam with hammerhead sharks last year, in Florida. It was wonderful!"

"There are hammerheads here, too, near one of the small islands," said Freddy. "**Tourists** don't go there."

"Why not?" asked Kristin. "Hammerheads are wonderful!"

"Would you like to go there?" said Freddy. "I can take you on Saturday. My dad has a boat."

dive /daɪv/ (v) When you *dive*, you swim a long way down under the water.
tourist /ˈtʊrɪst/ (n) *Tourists* are people on vacation. They usually visit different places and stay in hotels.

A world of sharks!

People love sharks because they are beautiful—and, at the same time, dangerous. They are about 450 million years old.

There are more than 350 different sharks and some can live for more than one hundred years. Some are as small as a pen. Others can be as long as six meters, but whale sharks are the biggest. Some are more than twelve meters long.

Some sharks are very dangerous. They can have as many as three thousand teeth.

Sometimes, but not often, sharks **attack** people. They can swim and turn quickly and easily, with the help of their fins. Other fish can stop and sleep, but not sharks. Sharks swim all the time—they never stop! Some sharks swim two thousand to three thousand kilometers each year. They can swim fast—about forty kilometers an hour. Some sharks swim with their mouths open and eat small animals and fish.

Sharks are intelligent. They can think, so they can **solve** problems. They have very good noses and strong eyes, and can see different colors. Sharks can hear very well, too. They can follow sounds and find smaller fish for their dinner. Sharks can eat a lot of food, but then they don't eat for a long time, sometimes for months.

Some sharks live near the ocean floor. Then they swim higher up in the water and look for smaller fish for their dinner.

The hammerhead is a strange shark. It has a large head, and one eye is a long way from the other eye. The dorsal fin is very big.

attack /əˈtæk/ (v/n) When an animal *attacks* you, it tries to hurt you.
solve /sɑlv/ (v) When you *solve* a problem, you find an answer.

2.1 Were you right?

Look at your answers to Activity 1.1.1 on page iv. Then finish each sentence below with one of these numbers:

12	350	100	3,000

1 There are more than .... different sharks.

2 Some are more than .... meters long.

3 They can have as many as .... teeth.

4 Some sharks can live for .... years.

2.2 What more did you learn?

1 Are these sentences right (✓) or wrong (✗)?

a ☐ The oceans are losing sharks.

b ☐ Some people want to protect ocean life.

c ☐ Sharks sleep on the ocean floor.

d ☐ They can't swim without their fins.

e ☐ Sharks can't see different colors.

f ☐ They can hear well and they follow sounds.

g ☐ Sharks only eat very big fish.

h ☐ Whale sharks are the biggest.

2 Who is speaking: Freddy or Kristin?

a "I swam with hammerheads last year." ....

b "My dad has a boat." ....

c "I came here because I want to dive." ....

d "Hammerheads are wonderful!" ....

e "There aren't any free places." ....

2.3 Language in use

1 Read the sentences in the box. Then finish the sentences with *has to*, *have to*, *had to*.

> Everybody **has to** pay now.
>
> Ed **had to** find the money.

a Freddy wanted to be a scientist so he .... work hard.

b College is expensive so everybody .... pay.

c Ed is a fisherman so he .... get up early.

d Fishermen .... go out in all weathers.

e The ocean is dangerous and they .... be careful.

f We all .... protect the oceans.

g Freddy knows that he .... help his family.

2 What do *you* have to do? Write two sentences.

....

....

2.4 What happens next?

Look at the pictures. What do you think is going to happen? Talk to other students.

CHAPTER 2

New Friends

"Too many sharks are dying. I want to protect the ocean. We have to make the world a better place!"

Angry students met outside Northcoast College yesterday

Freddy was angry. He didn't want to go on the shark-finning trip with his dad. He didn't want to help.

"Listen to me!" shouted Ed. "I'm doing this for you. Don't you understand?"

Freddy looked at his father. "I understand, Dad," he said. "Thank you. But we have to try something different. Too many sharks are dying. I want to protect the ocean. We have to make the world a better place!"

Freddy remembered photos of students in the streets, in newspapers.

Freddy left his father on the beach and walked quickly into the town. He wanted to find Kristin. Maybe they could go swimming and he could stop thinking about his problems.

Kristin was outside the store. She saw Freddy and called to him.

"Hi, Freddy! Do you have time for coffee? I have a lot of questions!"

"Questions about sharks, or about me?" Freddy asked, with a smile.

"Tell me about you first," said Kristin after they sat down.

"I was born here on the island," he began. "I played in the ocean every day and I loved it. Then, one day, some **scientists** arrived. They had a boat. I came down to the beach every day and talked to them. We made friends, and one day they took me on the boat with them. Clare Shepherd was with them. She's really famous, you know. She makes movies for World Television. She and the other scientists made a movie here: 'Ocean Life.' Maybe you saw it."

"Yes! I remember it! It was about different sharks! Was that here?" Kristin asked.

"Yes," said Freddy. "And after that I wanted to study and to be a scientist, too."

scientist /ˈsaɪəntɪst/ (n) Every day, *scientists* learn more new things about the world.

Sharks are different!

There are thirty families of sharks and each family is different. They are different colors. They eat different food. Their way of life is different.

Some sharks like cold water; some like warmer water. Some like the open ocean; some like to live near it. They don't usually like rivers, but some live in river **estuaries** and near beaches.

Not all sharks are born from eggs. Some sharks have **live** babies.

Some sharks swim a long way across the ocean; other sharks stay around one place.

These two sharks come from very different families.

Nurse sharks are very big—sometimes more than four meters long. They are not very dangerous, but they have more than one thousand

estuary /ˈɛstʃuˌɛri/ (n) Rivers run into an *estuary*, and then into the ocean.
live /laɪv/ (adj) A *live* baby can move when it is born.

teeth. Every fifteen days, they lose their old teeth and **grow** new teeth. Their teeth are interesting because they can turn around in the shark's mouth.

Nurse sharks **hunt** at night. In the day, they stay on the ocean floor. They live in the Atlantic and Pacific oceans. They like warm water and they stay in their families. When they are between fifteen and twenty years old, they start to **reproduce**. They can have about twenty or thirty baby sharks. These babies are born from eggs inside the mother.

The lemon shark's back is yellow. It has long, thin teeth and a young shark will lose them all every seven or eight days. Lemon sharks catch fish with their teeth. They eat other sharks, too. Lemon sharks can grow to three meters long. They live near the top of the water in different oceans in the world: in the Pacific Ocean around South America; in the Atlantic, near West Africa, and in the Gulf of Mexico. Sometimes they attack people.

grow /groʊ/ (v) When something *grows*, it gets bigger.
hunt /hʌnt/ (v) People *hunt* animals on foot, on horses, and in boats. They find an animal and then they kill it.
reproduce /ˌriprəˈdus/ (v) When an animal *reproduces*, it has babies.

3.1 Were you right?

Remember your answer to Activity 2.4. Then make sentences from the words below.

What is Kristin saying?

1 you time do have coffee for? 2 questions lot have I of a

....

....

3.2 What more did you learn?

Circle the right words in the sentences.

1 **a** They live *near the top of the water* / *on the ocean floor.*
b They like *warm* / *cold water.*
c They hunt *at night* / *in the afternoons.*
d Every fifteen *months* / *days* they grow new teeth.
e Their *teeth* / *ears* can turn around.

2 **a** They live *near the top of the water* / *on the ocean floor.*
b Their backs are *black* / *yellow.*
c They can be *3* / *30* meters long
d They have *short* / *long* teeth.
e They lose them about every *seven* / *seventeen* days.

3.3 Language in use

1 Look at the sentence in the box. Then finish the sentences below with past tense verbs.

I **came** down to the beach every day and **talked** to them.

a They .... a boat. (have) ( )

b That week, the scientists .... a movie: Ocean Life. (make) ( )

c I .... on the island. (born) (1)

d Every day, I .... in the ocean. (play) ( )

e One day, some scientists .... (arrive) ( )

f They .... me with them on their boat. (take) ( )

2 Now number the sentences, 1–6. What happened first? And then?

3.4 What happens next?

What do you think? Check (✔) the right answers.

1 In the next chapter Kristin will:

a ( ) go shark-finning with Freddy's family.

b ( ) tell Freddy about shark vacations.

c ( ) take Freddy to California.

2 How can Freddy pay for his place at college? Will he:

a ( ) get a job in the hotel?

b ( ) find money on the beach?

c ( ) try Kristin's idea?

CHAPTER 3

A Different Way

Things are changing here, but you have to understand the islanders. They don't have much money.

Kristin got up early. She liked running on the beach in the mornings. She put on her running shoes and went down to the ocean. When she got to the beach, she saw some women there, and a boat in the water. The boat came nearer and nearer. Kristin could see the fishermen on the boat. They had something in their hands.

"The men are throwing something to the women on the beach," thought Kristin, "but what?"

The women were busy. They didn't see her. Suddenly, Kristin stopped. She could see now. It was a shark fin!

She heard a noise behind her and turned around. It was Freddy.

"Go away, Kristin. I don't want you to see this," he said quietly.

"But Freddy, why are they doing this? Don't they know that the sharks will die?" Kristin answered angrily.

"Kristin, change comes slowly. Things are changing here, but you have to understand the islanders. They don't have much money. What can they do? They can make money from those fins."

The two new friends walked away from the beach. They didn't speak and they didn't look back at the beach. After some time, they came to a quiet place on the road and sat down under a tree.

Kristin turned to Freddy. "Listen to me, Freddy. I have an idea. Maybe it's the answer to the problems here."

"I'm listening," said Freddy.

"A lot of people love to dive," Kristin said, "and want to learn about life in the ocean. Do you know about Shark Week on TV? For seven days, they show movies about sharks and talk about them. My friend Gemma watches hours and hours of TV that week! She makes friends with other people on the Internet, and they plan shark vacations. They go to Palau and the Marshall Islands, to Hawaii and South Africa, to Mexico and Australia, and everywhere they see sharks.

"This island—your island—is beautiful. Divers will love it. We can talk to Pam and her parents at the hotel, and to your parents and your friends on the island. Some people can open their homes to visitors and make some money. Other people can start restaurants. Fishermen can take the tourists out in their boats. There will be work for everybody!"

"Yes," said Freddy slowly. "So we won't have to go on shark finning trips. The tourists will bring money to the island."

"That's right!" said Kristin.

Why are sharks endangered?

There are more than twenty-nine thousand different kinds of fish in our oceans. Most of them reproduce in great numbers with no problems. Sharks are different. Sharks grow old slowly and many do not reproduce for years. Often they don't have as many babies as other fish. They are in danger from people, too. Fishermen hunt them. This is not always difficult, because some sharks do not swim fast. The fishermen kill them or cut off their fins. Then they sell the fins and sometimes the meat.

In China, some people have shark fin soup at big family parties. People are learning more about sharks every day and a lot of restaurants do not have shark fin soup on the menu now. But is it too late?

Of course, some sharks die in accidents. Sometimes fishermen are trying to catch other kinds of fish, but they catch a shark. They don't always throw it back into the water. Sometimes big sharks hit ships.

Today, the numbers of sharks are falling and many kinds are now endangered.

The basking shark is the second biggest fish in the oceans. It can grow to ten meters. It has a very big mouth with many small teeth, a big nose, and very small eyes. It is not very dangerous. It moves slowly and enjoys warm water.

Dusky sharks are also very big fish. They can be four meters long and very heavy—more than 340 kilos! These sharks enjoy warm water and can swim more than one thousand kilometers from north to south.

People make soup with the fins of dusky sharks, so the numbers are falling. Maybe this will change, and we will see more dusky sharks in the future.

There are eight different kinds of hammerhead shark. (See the picture on page 5.) Most are not very dangerous. Hammerhead sharks often swim with one hundred or more other hammerheads. After four hundred million years in our oceans, they do not live in many places now. They have very big fins and fishermen like catching them.

4.1 Were you right?

1 Look back at Activity 3.4. Then look at these places for shark vacations. Which oceans (one or more) are they in or near?

Atlantic Indian Pacific

a Palau ....

b Hawaii ....

c South Africa ....

d Mexico ....

e Australia ....

2 Write these words in the sentences on the right.

dive plan sharks movie friends

4.2 What more did you learn?

1 Find the second part of the sentence.

a Today a lot of sharks are ...

b Fishermen hunt them ...

c Some restaurants have shark fin soup ...

d Now people are learning ...

1 for their fins.

2 more about sharks.

3 endangered.

4 on their menu.

2 Circle the right words.

a Basking sharks *can / don't* grow to 10 meters.

b They *are / are not* the biggest fish in the ocean.

c Dusky sharks *can / can't swim* more than 1,000 kilometers.

d Their numbers are *growing / falling.*

e Hammerheads *have / don't have* very big fins.

f They *often / never* swim with other hammerheads.

g Most *are / are not* very dangerous.

4.3 Language in use

1 **Look at the sentences in the box. Then put each adjective or adverb from the box in one of the sentences, a–g.**

"I don't want you to see this," he said **quietly**.

"Don't they know that the sharks will die?" Kristin answered **angrily**.

quiet	....	happy
....	slowly	....
....	easy	....
angrily	....	badly

a The women were tired so they worked ....slowly...... .

b The streets are very .... this morning.

c The fishermen shouted ....

d Their job wasn't ....

e My day ended .... because my train was very late.

f Do your homework .... and then we can go out.

g Her parents aren't .... about her boyfriend. They really don't like him.

2 **Now write the other adjectives and adverbs in the box.**

4.4 What happens next?

What do you think? Check (✔) the right answers.

1 ☐ Kristin and Freddy speak to Pam.

2 ☐ Kristin talks about Florida and her vacation there.

3 ☐ She talks about her idea of a Shark Week.

4 ☐ Pam says, "We can't do this on the island!"

5 ☐ Kristin says that it is going to be easy.

CHAPTER 4

Danger!

"That's really interesting," said Pam,
"and yes, we can do it here. But it won't be easy!"

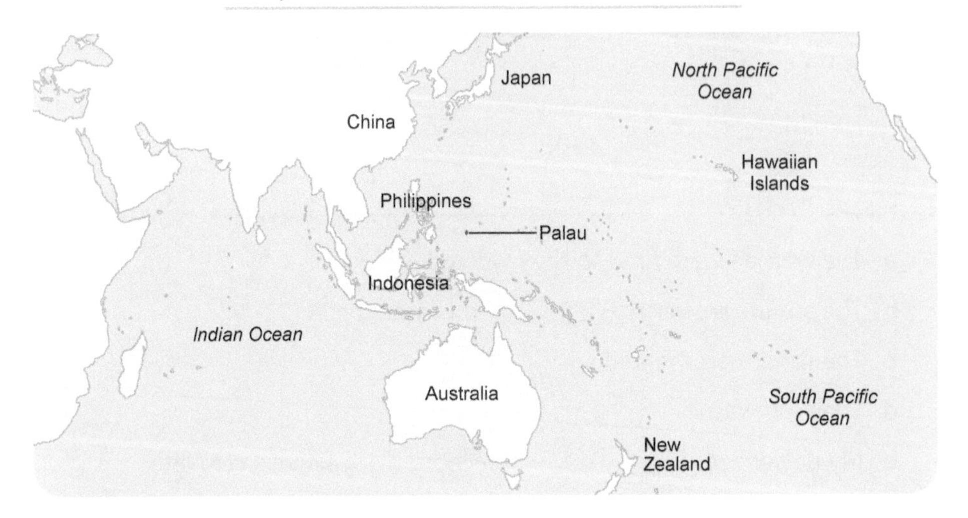

That evening, Kristin and Freddy met at the hotel. It was early and there were not many tourists, so they invited Pam to their table.

"Tell her about your idea," Freddy told Kristin. "She'll love it!"

"I'll tell you about Palau," Kristin began. "I was there last year. They have a Shark Week every year. It's really big! They have other shark study trips at different times, too. You can do that here!"

"Palau?" Pam said. "That's exciting! Is that near Australia?"

"Well, it's nearer the Philippines and Japan—in the Pacific Ocean."

"Tell me more about your vacation there," Pam said.

"People from sixteen different countries came," said Kristin. "There were about forty of us, all different ages. There were scientists, teachers, and doctors, too. They all love the ocean and they love sharks! In the morning, we went out on the boats. There was always somebody from the islands with us. That person taught us about the islands and about sharks."

"Are they protecting the sharks there?" asked Pam.

"Oh, yes, they are! They understand the problem. Nobody in Palau can catch them," said Kristin.

"Great! Did you dive at night?" asked Pam.

"No, we didn't," said Kristin, "but the evenings were wonderful. We all ate in the same restaurant and talked about our day. It was always exciting! Then there was usually a movie or something. We all had a lot of questions. We want to go back!"

"That's really interesting," said Pam, "and yes, we can do it here. But it won't be easy!"

"It wasn't easy in Palau," Kristin laughed. "Palau is a very young country."

"Do they have many shark attacks there?" asked Pam.

"No," said Kristin, "but when they happen, they're always in the newspapers. That's a problem, of course, because it makes tourists afraid."

Shark attack!

There are about sixty shark attacks around the world every year. People like to read about them—but the drive to the beach is more dangerous! Not all shark attacks end badly.

In June 1995, a white shark attacked Marco Flagg. Marco was thirty-one years old. He and two friends went on a trip to the ocean. The weather was good and they stayed out all day. In the afternoon, Marco was in the water when suddenly he saw a fin. It was the fin of a white shark.

Marco turned around and looked again. A big mouth full of teeth was behind him! He had to get out of the water. Suddenly, he felt the teeth in his arm, in his stomach, and then in his leg. Then he felt nothing. The shark went away. Marco swam back to the boat as fast as possible. His friends saw his cuts and took him to the hospital. He was very tired, but he was OK.

Jack Flint dives with sharks every day. People often ask him, "Is diving with sharks always dangerous?"

Well, no, it doesn't have to be dangerous, but you have to be careful. First, learn about the sharks. What kinds of sharks are in the ocean around you? Then, always remember—you are a visitor in the ocean. Go into the water slowly and quietly. Never swim to the sharks. They are wild animals. Sometimes they are afraid, or angry, and then they are dangerous. Never give food to sharks. Sharks hunt for food and they swim very near fish and fish ***parts*** *in the water. They can mistake a person's arm or leg for a fish. Then they will attack. And always dive with a friend. Remember—the ocean can be dangerous in many different ways. So have an exciting time and enjoy the sharks!*

part /pɑrt/ (n) A *part* of something is not all of it.

Which sharks are the most dangerous?

Not many sharks are really dangerous. Most sharks are usually more interested in other fish. The three most dangerous sharks are the great white shark, the bull shark, and the tiger shark.

The great white shark is the most dangerous of the three. It is not only white. It is also gray, and blue-gray, so we cannot see it very easily in the water.

Great white sharks live in different places in the world. Some live for forty years. The biggest are seven meters long, but usually they are a little smaller. Baby great whites grow inside their mothers, in eggs. When they are born, live, they are sometimes 2.5 meters long. Usually they are around 1.5 meters. After they are born, they swim away.

Great white sharks eat a lot of different things: live animals, and dead animals in the ocean, too. They have about three hundred long teeth, and some can swim twenty-five kilometers in an hour. In movies, they attack people on beaches, but this does not really often happen.

The bull shark lives in oceans and often swims near beaches. Bull sharks live in rivers and estuaries, too. You can find them around the Americas.

They swim fast, and have as many as three thousand teeth. Their teeth are interesting because they can turn in the shark's mouths. Bull sharks eat everything: birds, other sharks, and big fish—and sometimes tourists! You can see the dorsal fin above the water when it is near you.

Most people are afraid of tiger sharks. They are sometimes more than three meters long, and they can swim fast. They can attack people. In Hawaii, tiger sharks attack three or four people every year. Scientists there are studying the lives of these dangerous sharks, because they want to protect people. They sometimes find very interesting things in the sharks' stomachs: parts of cars, cameras, shoes, and a lot of different animals, too!

5.1 Were you right?

Look back at Activity 4.4. Then discuss Kristin's idea of Shark Week with another student. Is it a good plan? What problems can tourists bring?

5.2 What more did you learn?

1 Circle the right answers.

a In Palau, they ..... sharks.

eat kill protect

b Sharks ..... attack people.

sometimes never often

c The most dangerous shark is ..... .

the tiger shark the great white shark the bull shark

d Great white sharks can have ..... teeth.

300 3,000 30,000

e When they are born, they are sometimes ..... meters long.

1.5 2.5 5.2

2 Look at the pictures. What happened first? Write the numbers 1–6. Then tell Marco Flagg's story.

.3 Language in use

Look at the sentences in the box. Then write *so*, or *when* in the sentences below.

There were not many tourists, **so** they invited Pam to their table.

Marco was in the water **when** suddenly he saw a fin.

1 They had some free time .... they went out on the boat.

2 They were near the island .... they saw something on the beach.

3 It looked interesting .... they went nearer.

4 .... they arrived on the beach, it moved!

5 It didn't look dangerous .... they weren't afraid.

6 Suddenly it made a loud noise .... they stopped.

7 They took out their cameras .... it flew into a tree.

8 The strange bird was too high .... the pictures weren't good.

.4 What happens next?

Look at the first three pictures in Chapter 5. What do you think? Check (✔) the right sentences.

1 ☐ There are dead sharks in the ocean.

2 ☐ Two policemen see Ed's boat.

3 ☐ Ed is with his family.

4 ☐ They are shark finning.

5 ☐ The policemen take Ed back to the island.

6 ☐ Ed has a plan, and the police want to hear it.

Interesting Plans

"I had a call about dead sharks in the ocean. Who killed them?"
"I don't know, but it wasn't us!"

Rod worked for the ocean police. His office was across the island from Freddy's family. The police protected the ocean around the island.

One morning, he was in his office when somebody called him.

A man spoke: "Excuse me. Is that the ocean police office? There's a shark finning boat ..."

Rod sat up. This was interesting! "Where?" he asked.

"South of Barras Beach. We're divers. We arrived there at about eight thirty and saw dead sharks in the water. They were hammerheads. There was a boat about a kilometer south of the beach," said the man.

"Did you see the people on the boat?" asked Rod.

"No, we didn't see anybody. We came back quickly. We wanted to call you," answered the man.

"Good. Thank you," said Rod, and asked for his name.

This was not a new problem for Rod, but it was difficult. Was it Ed's boat? Ed was his friend, and Ed had a boat near Barras Beach.

Rod went into the office next door and shouted to another policeman.

"Hey, Wilson! We're going on a trip! I'll see you at the boat in two minutes."

"OK, I'm ready," said Wilson. He jumped up and put on his jacket.

Rod called Ed's number, but there was no answer. Five minutes later, the two men climbed into the police boat and went south to Barras Beach. The police boat was fast—faster than Ed's boat, and the other fishing boats.

Suddenly, Rod saw Ed's boat on the water. He was with his family.

"Ed!" called Rod. "Bring your boat here. We want to talk to you."

He climbed onto Ed's boat. "Where are you going? What are you

doing?" he asked.

Ed looked at Rod. "Hi, Rod. What's wrong? I'm here with the family. We're looking for a diving place."

"Ed," said Rod, "were you near Barras Beach earlier this morning?"

"No," said Ed. "Listen, Rod. We're planning something interesting, and you're going to like the idea."

"I want to hear your plan Ed," said Rod, "but we have a problem near

Barras Beach. I had a call about dead sharks in the ocean. Who killed them?"

"I don't know, but it wasn't us!" Ed told him. "Shark finning is wrong. I understand that now and I'm not going to do it again."

"That's great, Ed, but think. Did you see a boat on its way south?" asked Rod.

Ed looked at his family. Nobody saw anything.

Rod jumped back into his boat. "OK. Let's meet tonight at the hotel," he shouted. You can tell me your plan then."

That evening, Rod was tired but happy. After a difficult morning, he and Wilson caught the shark finning boat. The men were at the police station. Now it was time for a drink with Ed and his family and the young American girl. He listened to their plans for more tourists on the island. When Kristin spoke about Palau, Rod smiled at her.

"Are you going to help?" he asked.

"Of course," said Kristin, "but will *you* help, too? Everybody on the island has to work with us."

"Shark tourists will be good for everybody. We have some hotels, restaurants and boats now," said Freddy. "But there will be more when there are more tourists."

"And, of course, we have the sharks, too," said Ed, with a smile. "So let's protect them—not kill them."

"Yes, maybe this idea can solve the problem of shark finning," said Rod. He thought about his morning with Wilson. He couldn't forget the ugly picture of those dead sharks in the ocean. "Let's discuss this with Pam and her parents, and with the other islanders. We'll do it tomorrow!"

Most people were happy with the idea, but Freddy's family was very excited.

"More tourists on the island will bring money," said Freddy, "and we'll meet a lot of new people."

His mother loved the idea. She taught in the school in the town.

"We're studying sharks now," she said to Freddy. "The children can make a book about the different sharks for the tourists. And they can put some pages on the Internet."

"That's right. The hotels can use them and tell visitors about our plans," said Ed.

Big and beautiful:

Today, the whale shark is the biggest fish and the biggest shark in our oceans. It is not a whale, but it is very big. It can be as long as fourteen meters. It has the biggest mouth of all sharks, and three thousand small teeth. It only eats very small fish, so it doesn't use its teeth.

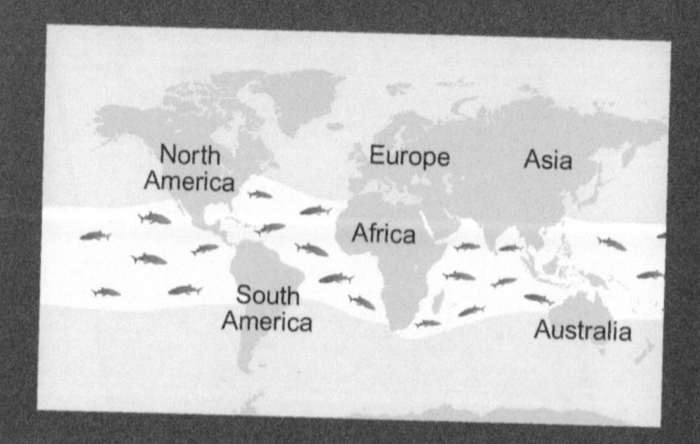

the whale shark

Other sharks have their mouth below their head, but this shark's mouth is at the front. It has small eyes, two dorsal fins and two pectoral fins.

Whale sharks have live babies, sometimes ten each year for thirty years. Some baby whale sharks can be a little more than half a meter long.

Whale sharks can live for more than one hundred years. They live in warm water near beaches or in the open ocean, in oceans around the world. They like to stay near the top of the water. They swim with their mouths open and drink six thousand liters of water every hour! They can swim and eat at the same time. They swim slowly, only about five kilometers an hour. They are not dangerous and they do not attack people. People love to dive and swim with whale sharks.

6.1 Were you right?

Look at your answers to Activity 5.4. Then look at the words below. What is Ed saying?

Put the words in his sentences.

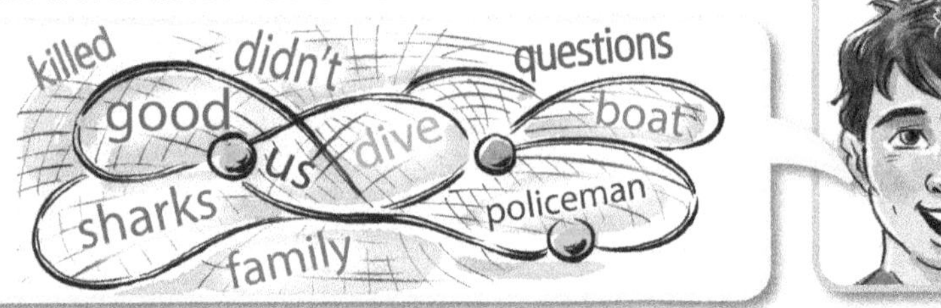

I was on the [1] .... with Kristin and my [2] .... I saw Rod and another [3] .... They came and asked [4] .... There were some dead [5] .... in the water. Who [6] .... them? We [7] .... know. It wasn't [8] ....! We only wanted to [9] ...., and we found a [10] .... place for that.

6.2 What more did you learn?

What do you know about the whale shark? Finish the sentences.

6.3 Language in use

Look at the sentences in the box. Then circle the right words in the sentences below.

He was in his office when **somebody** called him.

"We didn't see **anybody**."

1 There was *nothing / anything* on the boat.
2 But *somebody / anybody* killed the sharks!
3 The fins were *everywhere / nowhere* on the beach.
4 They had to do *everything / something*!
5 *Somebody / Nobody* had any ideas.
6 Suddenly, *everything / anything* was quiet.
7 A fisherman arrived from *anywhere / nowhere*.
8 "Listen, *anybody / everybody!*" he said, "I have the answer."

6.4 What happens next?

Discuss these questions. What do you think?

1 Look at the pictures on pages 36 and 37.

- **a** Who can you see in the pictures?
- **b** What are they doing?

2 What will happen at the end of the story?

- **a** There is a big party in town. What is the party for?
- **b** Freddy is going away. Why? Where do you think he is going? Is he happy about it?
- **c** At the party Freddy meets somebody from the past. Who?

3 Scientists are working in the oceans today.

- **a** What are they learning about sharks?
- **b** How can we protect life in our oceans?

CHAPTER 6

A Look at the Future

There is no more talk on the island now about shark finning. The sharks are too important to the islanders.

A year later, there is a big party in town. It is the end of the first Shark Week on the island. The hotels are full of tourists and there are people from the newspapers and some TV people, too.

Shark Week was wonderful and everybody had a great time. There were no shark attacks! There is no more talk on the island now about shark finning. The sharks are too important to the islanders.

That day's boat trip was the best, and Kristin is putting up photos of the trip on the wall of the restaurant in Pam's parents' hotel.

The small hotel is bigger now and a lot of new people are working there. Today the cooks and waiters are going to be busy. They are making food and drinks for the tourists and other visitors. Every tourist on the island will be there. The teachers and students from the school are coming, too. But first some people from "Protect Sharks Now" are going to talk to everybody. They will talk about sharks, the ocean, and the future.

Freddy is going to go to college in February. He will come home for vacations and help with Shark Week each year. Sometimes he will come for shark study trips, too. One day he wants to work with the scientists and study sharks.

Freddy hears the sound of a car. Then Pam and the scientists come into the hotel. A lot of people want to talk to the scientists and there isn't much time. Freddy helps them with their bags. Suddenly, he stops. "I know that woman!" he thinks. "She's older and grayer, but the face is the same."

Freddy remembers that boat trip, when he was only eleven years old. Scientists took photos and then they made a movie. When Dr. Shepherd talked to him about the ocean and the movie, it changed his life. And now she is here again!

When everybody is sitting down, Dr. Shepherd begins to talk.

Good afternoon, everybody. Here I am again on this beautiful island. I have some pictures and a movie for you and I'll try to answer your questions. Let's begin.

How and why do sharks find their way from place to place?

Next to a mountain under the ocean near Mexico, hammerhead sharks meet in large numbers in the day. Every night, they swim out to the open ocean and look for food. They swim in a **line** for about twenty kilometers. Then, they turn and swim back in the same line. They can't see the sky, and they can't see the floor of the ocean. So how do they do it?

We don't know, but scientists are learning every day. Now, look at this.

When Dr. Shepherd's talk ends, a lot of people have questions for her. Freddy has a question, too.

He thanks her for her talk and then says, "You came to this island before. I was only a boy then. Do you remember?"

"Wait! Oh, yes, of course I remember. You were very young. You wanted to come with us on the boat," says Dr. Shepherd.

"Yes, that's right, and I did," said Freddy. "You took me with you and I loved it."

"Do you want to come with us again?" the scientist asks.

"Yes—yes, please!" Freddy answers. "Thank you! But first, the party!"

Work with two friends. Have these conversations.

1

Student A	You go to a restaurant. Shark fin soup is on the menu. You are very angry. Talk to the waiter/waitress about this.
Student B	You are the waiter/waitress. You do not choose the menu. Tell the customer.
Student C	It is your restaurant. The waiter/waitress is having problems. Speak to him/her and the customer.

2

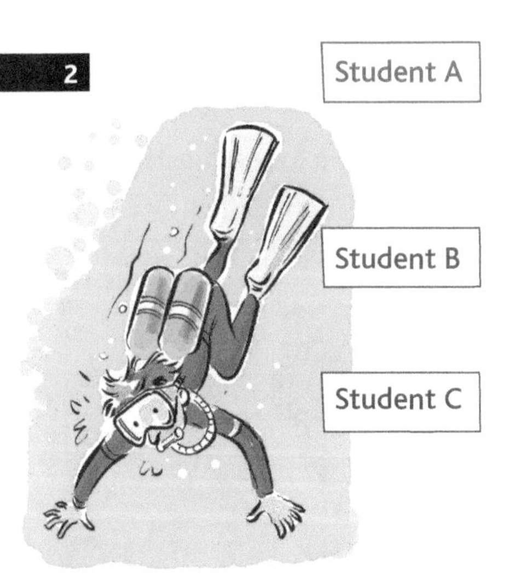

Student A	You are a diver. You work in a hotel and you are taking some students on a boat trip. The ocean can be dangerous. Tell the students why.
Student B	You and your best friend are going on the trip. You want to dive and see sharks. Listen and ask questions.
Student C	You are Student B's best friend. You are afraid of big fish. You can swim but not very well. When you hear the diver's talk, you don't want to dive. Tell the diver and your friend.

3 You are watching the movie "Jaws" and having a conversation.

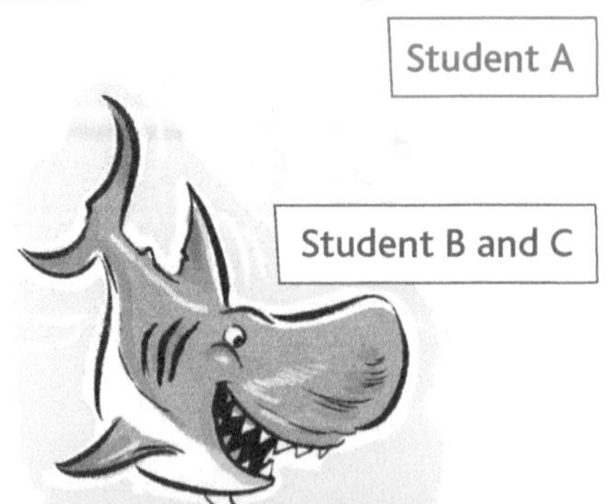

Student A	You are afraid of sharks. They are all very dangerous. Sharks always attack people and you don't like them! Tell your friends.
Student B and C	You know a lot about different sharks. Your friend is wrong. Tell your friend about sharks and change his/her ideas.

1 You are going to talk about sharks to a class of older students. What are you going to say? Choose photos from this book and write two or three sentences about each photo in your notebook. You only have twenty minutes, so use about eight pictures.

2 You are taking some friends to Palau. It is their first trip to the islands. You have some notes. What are you going to tell them? Write your talk in your notebooks.

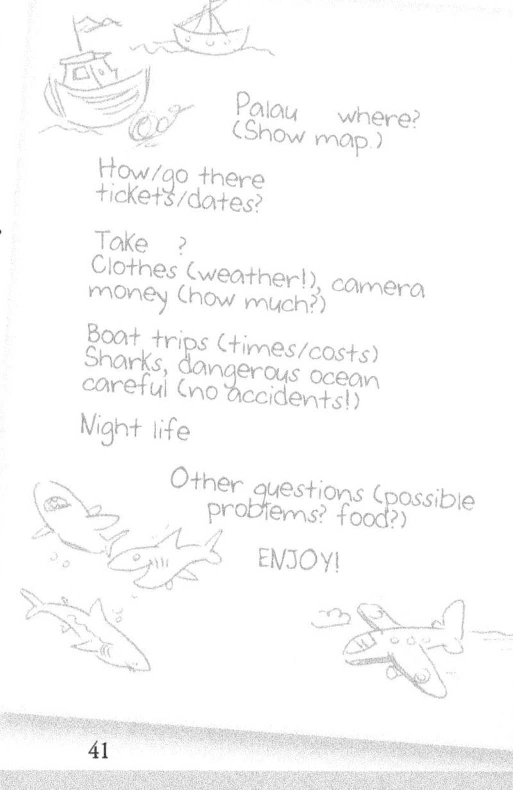

1 How can *you* protect the oceans? Work with two or three other students.

1 Number the ideas below, 1–7. 1 is the most important.

a ◯ Never eat very small fish. They have to reproduce first.

b ◯ Don't throw away bottles and bags. There are a lot of them in the oceans, and they are dangerous. Fish can eat small parts of them and die. Use them again and again.

c ◯ Don't make the beach dirty. Take your trash home with you.

d ◯ People make things from ocean life and sell them. Don't buy them. Leave ocean life in the ocean.

e ◯ Think about your dog or cat's food. Some animal food comes from fish, and in some places fishermen are taking a lot of fish from the oceans.

f ◯ Talk to your friends about the oceans. Then, with them, plan an Ocean Day in your town.

g ◯ What is in the ocean near you? Learn more on the Internet.

2 Write down two more ideas.

....

....

2 You are going to have an Ocean Day in your town. How are you going to do this? Make notes.

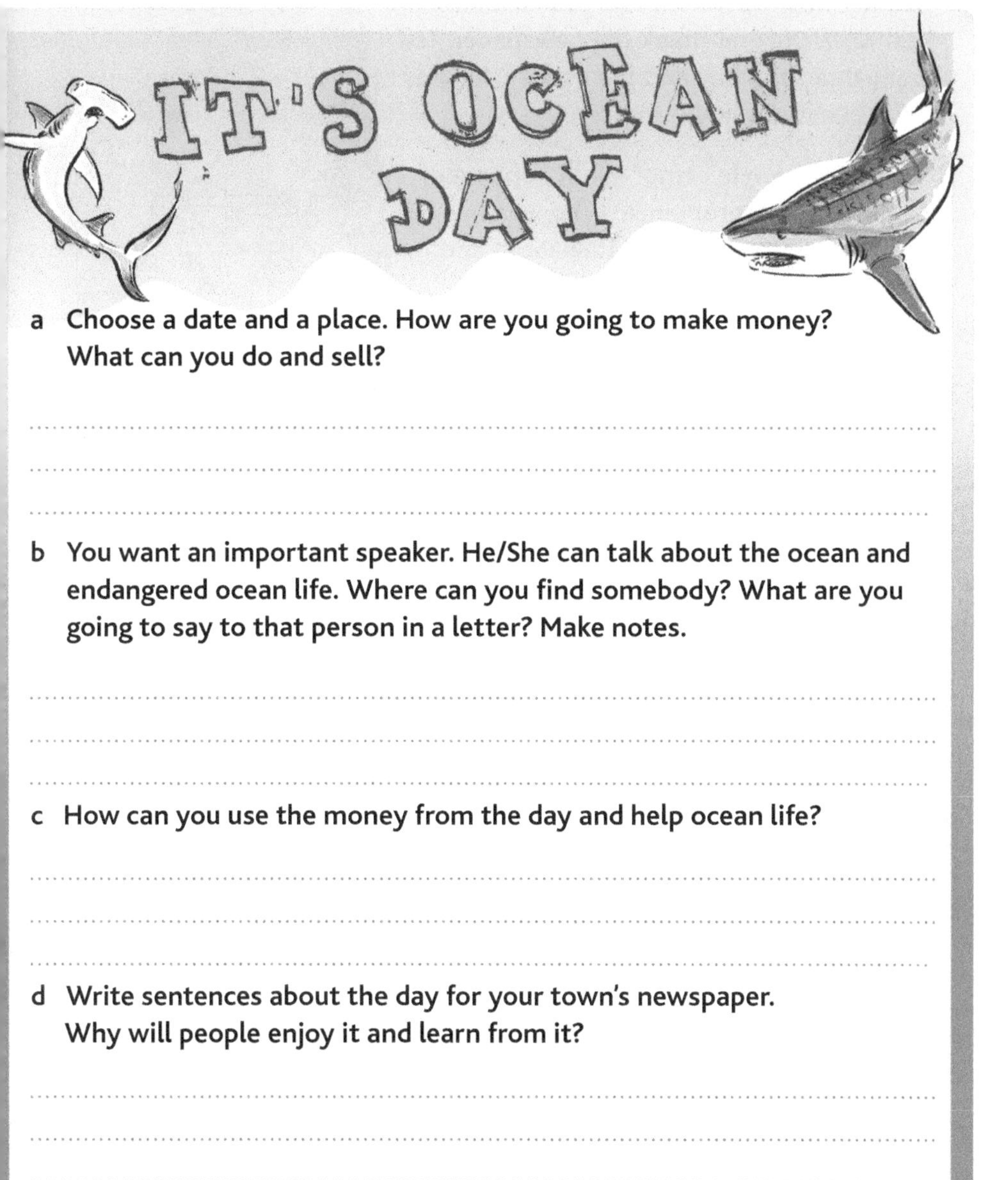

a Choose a date and a place. How are you going to make money? What can you do and sell?

....

....

....

b You want an important speaker. He/She can talk about the ocean and endangered ocean life. Where can you find somebody? What are you going to say to that person in a letter? Make notes.

....

....

....

c How can you use the money from the day and help ocean life?

....

....

....

d Write sentences about the day for your town's newspaper. Why will people enjoy it and learn from it?

....

....

....

3 **The day was wonderful and you now have $2,000! Write and thank the newspaper. Tell them about the day and the money. Answer these questions in your letter:**

How many people came? What happened? Were there any problems? Who was the speaker? What did he/she talk about and where did he/she come from? What did visitors say about the day? What was the best part? How much money did you get? What are you going to use it for? Will you do this again?